Sunshine & Darkness

A Collection by Thomas Dobson (Poet Dobby)

Hello, my name is Thomas or Poet Dobby and please allow me this brief introduction to this collection of my poetry focusing on depression, darkness and other things.

I have been battling my personal demons for years now, some days they almost consume me and on others we just snuggle.

For me personally, depression doesn't hit me every day, sometimes it washes over me in a wave of sadness and some days I feel like I could fly.

That's one of the reasons I wanted to compile this book and hopefully reach people that believe they don't have a voice or even a choice, believe me when I say this, you matter to me and I am happy you have picked up my book.

I may not have the answers for you but I hope to give you an insight into my ongoing battle.
If one can relate to any one of these poems or my ramblings afterwards then I have done my job as a poet and more importantly as a human.

If you ever feel like you need a friend and safe place without judgement, the Samaritans have helped me immensely as well as many other organisations around the world.

Anyway that is enough of my rambling and I hope you find solace in the raw pieces you'll find from here on in.

They won't all be about depression; I've tried to weave some positivity into it as well. Hence the name of the book.

The Path

I closed my eyes
Just for a minute
In that moment
I saw possibilities infinite
Paths spewed out
Forking away
Like a tree
Whose branches sway
I stepped out onto a branch
And only saw pain
I retracted quickly
Back to the main
Onto a different path now
This one full of joy
Like from what I remember
When I was just a boy
This overcame me
And so I retreated
Back to the trunk
Feeling completely defeated
If the path of pain
Was just too strong
And the path of joy
Felt so wrong
Could I find a greyer path?
One filled with every possibility?
Even for me, someone who
Suffers from intractability
I woke up
Sleepy from that doze
But the message still in my mind
Of which path I chose...

Who am I?

Maybe I'm different
Or something unique
Maybe I'm misunderstood
Or just a freak
Maybe my wiring
Was completed wrong
Maybe I'm just weak
And not strong
Maybe I'm an old soul
Not destined for this decade
Maybe I'm to blame
For every mistake I've made
Maybe I'm too trusting
Or just searching for my clan
Maybe I'm just a scared little boy
Trying to be a man
Maybe I'm all this
And so much more
Maybe I'll just have another drink
Sitting crossed legged on the floor…

Just know that you have the power to be whatever you choose to be, I spent years trying to even be content with who I am and develop an identity.
Personally for me I found social media blackouts to be helpful and television as well but we all have different things that help us.

Blackout

My soul is torn
Depression reborn
My heart is ripped
Confidence snipped
My body's a shell
Oh well
My skin is scratched
Becoming detached
My mind is fragmented
Unprecedented
My eyes no longer see
Any guarantee
Muscles begin to tighten
My future frightens
My veins run cold
With tales untold
My blood crimson red
Tourniquet bled
Death is my last shout
Blackout...

So many times (too many to count), I have seriously considered taking my own life but somehow, I'm still here...

How I wish

How I wish
I could say goodbye
How I wish
I didn't cry
How I wish
For dreamless nights
How I wish
Not to wake up to frights
How I wish
I could rewind
How I wish
I could silence my mind
How I wish
Upon a falling star
How I wish
You weren't too far
Oh how I wish
As a penny drops into the well
I truly wish
I wasn't this broken shell…

If you had one wish, just one, what would it be?

Razor blade words

Another verbal assault
Starts a new war
The barrage doesn't cease
Even with me on the floor
Assault after assault
Have you found my Achilles heel?
I guess words can cut
Is it easier not to feel?
Slaps and punches
Now them I can take
But your razor blade words
On my soul they rake
So please grant me peace
So I can rest
Before the next round
Of your vocal test...

Abuse is abuse, no matter who it comes from.

Dirge of Dobby

I woke today
If indeed you can wake
After a sleepless night
How many more can I take?
Because when I do sleep
Nightmares and memories haunt
When I'm awake
Demons taunt
The only way this ceases
Is when ink meets paper white
Then my blood flows through my pen
Spilling blood in the form of ink
Slowly making me whole again
But how many poems must I compile?
Until my soul is purged
Or will I write that final piece
To be read as my dirge?

With this piece I've tried saying that we all need a release from our suffering.
Mine comes from writing but I have drunk in the past as well, both seem to give me a hangover but writing doesn't cause me physical harm.
I urge you to find a release that isn't detrimental to yourself or to others, I won't pretend to know what exactly will help though.

Today

Today I failed
Today I bled
Today I gave in
Today I fed
Yesterday's demons
Yesterday's pain
Today I cut
For tomorrow's gain
Every slice
Every claret river
Brings me salvation
Each with its own shiver
This razor blade and bottle
Offer me direction
And each slit
Stems my soulful infection…

After going months without cutting myself, I failed.

Warriors Demise

Eternal winter
No end in sight
Snow blanketing
From left to right
Encasing my world
Leaving me isolated
Standing in the cold
Completely deflated
Once a proud warrior
Now a quivering wreck
Longing for days of summer
As I continue on my soul's trek
Will I find redemption?
An awakening of my fire?
Or shall I simply vanish
On life's cruel funeral pyre?

It feels like my depression has me locked in an eternal winter with no end in sight, luckily I have Hot chocolate...

The game of life

*A roll of the dice
A turn of the card
Another chip down
The game of life is hard
Lady luck eludes me
My rabbits paw doesn't work
Serendipity long departed
The house is a jerk
Or maybe I'm cursed
Destined to be without luck
One last hand is played
Ah fuck
The final card dealt
A losing hand
After that godforsaken turn
Solemnly I try to stand
My legs barely holding
A weight bears down
The end seems nigh
I lost my crown
My composure as well
Overwhelmed by strife
I break down and crumble
I just lost in the game of life…*

*In the game of life, does the house always win?
Can we turn the tide and recoup our losses?*

True

*How can something you love
Hurt you so much?
Something you've dreamt of
Cause nightmares at a touch?
Something of pure beauty
Bring so much pain?
Oh my beautiful disaster
You're forever in my hearts frame
You were my freedom
Yet confined me as well
My one true heaven
And my one true hell...*

*Let me leave this unanswered and instead ask you what this poem means to you?
It seems everyone reads and interprets this differently.*

Society

Societal pressure
Forces me to smile
Even though I haven't
Felt this way in a while
People think I'm angry
Because my looks stern
Oh, dear society
You have much to learn
They say I should be happy
Because I have a job and a flat
But if those make you happy
To you I tip my hat
We treat unhappiness
And depression like it's contagious
But surely breaking the societal norm
Should be considered courageous?
But no we're treated like outcasts
Like lepers and freak shows
All I ask is when you see me
Don't look down your nose...

Too often I have been told to cheer up or smile when in fact I have actually been happy.

Christmas Spirit

Ooh look
I got a shiny handbag
Ooh look
I forgot to take off the price tag
Ooh look
At all the presents I bought
Ooh look
At all the glances I've caught
Ooh look
At all the food I've eaten
Ooh look
I've added cinnamon to sweeten
Ooh look
There's Mr. humbug
Ooh look
No one wants to give him a hug
Ooh look
That man hasn't got a smile upon his face
Ooh look
He's at home staring at an empty space…

I wrote this one after a Christmas passed without seeing anyone all holiday and chose to work as I had no invites and contemplated if life was meant for me.
It was a very dark time for me and a real low point but honestly it made me realise that there are those that were there for me and those that just said so.

Star

Little star
Shining bright
Up above
In a sky of night
Do you look at us?
And see our petty ways
How frivolous we are
As we lumber through our days?
When there's such beauty up above
Why would you?
So shine on little star
And leave us few
To our petty squabbles
As I gaze upon your light
At the end of my days
I think of you every night
As I sit and wonder
I even talk to you at times
I just hope you know that down here
Someone watches your little shines
That you give me hope just knowing
How miniscule my problems are?
So please shine on
My little star...

Have you stopped and stared up at the night sky lately? I live in a big city so I whenever I get out to the countryside, I try and make the most of it.

Human

Do you ever feel low or sad?
As if smiling is bad?
Like it's a true crime to grin?
Like being happy is a sin?
Slowly the depression creeps
And quietly your heart weeps
It works up your spine to your eyes
They water quicker than you realise
Then with nowhere left to go
They suddenly overflow
Like a river bursting its banks
But don't offer me a tissue, I'll be fine thanks
I sometimes just need to let the tears fall
I am only human after all...

Have you ever just felt the need to cry?
I wish someone told me as a child that it was okay to cry.
Instead I always got told that boys don't cry.
Can we change this please?

True path

Am I the instrument of my own demise?
How many times can I truly rise?
It's like every time my legs buckle
The Devil gives a little chuckle
I feel his pull more than ever
Like I'm stuck to him on a tether
But then I feel God's touch
Oh how I need it so much
Constantly I feel like I'm walking two paths
God looking disapproving and devil just laughs
He knows he's winning this round
To drag me just below ground
When I want nothing more than to be great
And be allowed through that pearly gate
But I suppose even angels can become tainted
Even after being sainted
Is this destined to be my way?
I mean even Lucifer was an angel lead astray
Destined to forever feels God's wrath
Is this really my true path?

After turning away from Catholicism as a teenager, I have always had this war going on inside me.

Coffee Date

Depression isn't purely negative
Sometimes good days appear
Survive the downpour
The sunshine is near
Believe me friend
I'll stand there under the typhoon
For the tide will turn one night
As we stare up at the full moon
If you cannot see the light at the end
Then that's okay
I'll hold the torch and together
We will see a brighter day
One day over coffee
We will reminisce
About how we both survived the darkness
And crawled out of the abyss…

I was reminded of the words from my old man who used to always tell me that "we never know the impact we have on others so if you can be nice, then be nice, if you can be generous then be generous and if you can help someone" well you get the point.
In a world full of darkness, be a light for someone, trust me when I say that helping others has always staved my demons off for a while, coincidence?

My only true friend

*I wanted to write a happy rhyme
But that's not the case this time
Is it better to shout?
Or to block the world out?
I instead chose my notebook
Whilst sitting in a cranny or nook
My headphones on with music turned up
As I sip coffee from my favourite coffee cup
My words spill onto my page
Just sadness, no happiness or rage
To make it worse I cannot pinpoint my sorrow
Maybe I'm just dreaming of a better tomorrow?
That's speaking metaphorically
Will I be happier then? Asked rhetorically
Or will I continue to only trust in my pen
With the thoughts that echo over again
Please don't ask if I'm okay or fine
As that only brings out a tired line
Maybe my notepad is my only true friend
Who guards all my thoughts I've ever penned...*

I used to get caught up with trying to be insta-famous and for a long while I only put poems out that I thought might gain me likes or follows (I mean who honestly would want to be followed in real life?).
Only when I started sharing my darker poems did I start to realise the need for books like this and how surrounded I was with people who actually live with demons and depression.
For the best part of half my life, I truly believed that my notepad and pen were my only friends other than the demons that I gained along the way, how wrong I was.

Butterfly Effect

If I could rewind time
And talk to my younger self
I'd tell him to focus
On his mental health
I'd warn him of trials
But not in detail
As the butterfly effect
May instead derail
Somehow they may have become worse
And shattered me beyond repair
I may have been unsalvageable
Locked inside an eternal nightmare
A constant battleground
Far off the beaten track
So after this thought
Would I still choose to go back?

In this poem I felt a little reflective and considered what I would say to my younger self.
With the butterfly effect in mind, I'm not so sure if I would go back, especially when I could stand in the mirror and tell my present self these things and shape my future from here on.

Now don't get me wrong, install hate standing in front of the mirror and talking to myself (it makes me feel like a mad man) but it does help me.

London Town

My favourite bench
Sitting by the river
The cold snaps
I suppress a shiver
I wrap my scarf closer
I turn my music down
And listen to the sounds
Of my beloved London Town
Couples pass
Joggers run by
No stars' tonight
As clouds drift in the night sky
I probably look strange
With a pen and notepad
But times like this remind me
That London isn't just a fad
It's not for everyone
My wonderful city
And even though some memories
Are filled with pity
I still love you
All that's left to say
London you look just as beautiful
At night as you do in the day…

With this poem, I pay a little homage to my first love, London.
She has tested me, taught me and pushed me to my limits but she has always provided inspiration and let me know that even if I feel alone, I'm truly not.

Cutting Ties

Shiny new scissors bought
Now I begin cutting ties
No reasons needed
And no goodbyes
Cutting negativity feels great
Contacts on the floor aplenty
So if you don't hear from me again
I wish you well in 2020
I won't tell you my resolutions
I won't whisper my goals
My happiness is in my own hands
And I'm the one who controls
So if your message is left on seen
Just know I never gave up on you
I just never saw a reason to stay
Apart from a few
So pull up a chair
And some popcorn to eat
Because only from afar
You will see my life become sweet...

So many times over the years I cut myself rather than cutting ties and I don't mean suits.
Never underestimate the power of removing negative people from your life whilst you're healing yourself.
I have recently discovered and implemented this so maybe soon I will start to reap the benefits.

A Poet

"Please no more"
I cry into my pillow
Dripping with sweat
"Please, I cannot carry this cargo"
My demons keep taunting
"You failed at life"
My demons press onwards
"Go and grab that knife"
My cries turn into wails
As blade meets flesh
"Yes, I knew you'd do it"
The wound feels fresh
Black ichor oozes
My demons cackle with glee
I stare down at the fluid pouring
"Your blood is ink you see"
I slice again hoping to drain my life
"Heh, it's not that easy and you know it"
I choke out "I'm sorry"
"I didn't know it was this hard to be a poet" …

From time to time I have found myself wondering if I'm meant to be a poet, I grew up at a time that creativity wasn't meant for men, we were meant to build things or break things down. In a way that's what I do with poetry, I build people up but break myself into pieces.
Even after practising with poetry for years now, I still struggle with how to write without it being detrimental to myself but as they say "tomorrow is a new day".

A boxer's life

Left, Right, Uppercut
I take a knee
Another combination hits
My eyes can barely see
I find my feet again
A jab explodes my nose
Claret has smeared my face
Is this how it goes?
An uppercut finds my chin
My legs give way
I hit the floor
"Stay down kid"
"You cannot take any more"
I rise bloody, battered and bruised
Barely holding out
The bell rings to stop this round
Is this really what life is about?

I was always told to roll with the punches but for how long can you do this? When do you throw in the towel? When do you say "No more"?

Reset

I'm on my knees pleading
Both wrists bleeding
Please stop my suffering and pain
And in exchange accept this claret rain
Take it as the price for my soul
This life has finally taken its toll
Forgive me for my cowardice
Allow me this sacrifice
If I'm reborn I'll be better
Live my life to your letter
So as the razor blade continues to grate
I silently wonder if I'll get my clean slate?

Another rhetorical question as I know the answer is no but I still find myself asking if I can start over and reset.

In these moments I either decide to sleep (or at least try), I write or I used to drink.
I now know that one of these was extremely detrimental to me in more ways than one so I chose (begrudgingly) to give up drinking.

Towers

Together we can build towers
Yet cannot rewind hours
Tomorrow's a gift and not a given right
Because of that I'll always fight
Giving up has never been a real option
Feel free to give this idea adoption
Fight, fight and fight some more
Don't give up till you're six feet under the floor
Even when you don't feel strong
I'll carry you along
With my words or muscle
I'll save you from life's hustle
From depression decline
Just send me a sign
I'll be there as soon as I can
And together we shall hatch a plan
Just remember to hold my hand
Until on your own you can stand…

My friend, take my hand…

Drowning

Dark rum on the rocks
My demons delight
With each sip
I lose the fight
My demons grow stronger
With each mouthful taken
Each mindful assault
Leaving me shaken
I pour another
They seem amused
With each gulp
I'm mentally abused
Still I drink
Numb to the pain
As old demons rise
Long thought slain
Another glass is downed
Now an empty bottle
I'm the butt of their jokes
A jester in his mottle
Except no-one here is laughing
These are the tears of a clown
And into this fresh glass
I drown...

This right here is one of my raw pieces about how I used to drink bottles of rum to numb my pain.
Please take it from someone who has been there, there is no salvation at the bottom of the bottle.

Rain drop

*A single droplet of rain
Trickles down my window
I wonder how far it has travelled
And where it will go
Will it desire to join others?
And turn into a river
Or does it desire to be alone
And on its own slither
Does it hold a destiny?
Or even a plan
Then I wonder if this raindrop
Is a representation of man?*

*I sometimes find myself contemplating life (can you tell?).
Are we fate bound?
Our destinies predefined?
Or can we change the status quo and shape it to our will?*

*I try to make my own destiny and make things happen
but likewise, I also enjoy lazy days.
Life is all about balance right?*

<u>Me</u>

Tears
Long run dry
Eyes
That refuse to cry
Lips
That forget the word friend
Thoughts
That seem to have no end
Fingers
Longing to feel
Heart
Fallen ill
Brain
Long infected
Body
No longer erected
Cheeks
Sullen deep
Soul
Coma like sleep
Hands
No longer holding
A man
Slowly colding...

All of these things make up me.

Warrior's demise

Eternal winter
No end in sight
Snow blanketing
From left to right
Encasing my world
Leaving me isolated
Standing in the cold
Completely deflated
Once a proud warrior
Now a quivering wreck
Longing for summer days
As I continue my soul's trek
Will I find redemption?
An awakening of my fire
Or shall I simply vanish
On life's cruel pyre?

I always imagined my battle as this grand finale in a coliseum when in reality I just cry in my bathtub…

Red Flags

It's all in the details
No matter how small
The red flags
I'm just a fool

It's all in the details
I was blinds folded
I thought you'd change
But every time I was scolded

It's all in the details
Why didn't I leave?
Now my heart breaks
And I cannot breathe

It's all in the details
Or so they say
Please tell me I'll be fine
One day...

I wrote this piece using a prompt by a friend and focused it on a past abusive relationship.
With hindsight, I realised there were many red flags that, at the time, I missed.

Love is gone

Love is gone
Flown away
On the wind
Far over the bay

Love is gone
Migration begun
And here I stand
Loved by none

Love is gone
No refund allowed
I'm broken inside
No longer proud

Love is gone
And so are you
Forever alone
Feeling blue

Love is gone
I lost my chance
Of our first kiss
And first dance…

Do we need love to feel validated?
What if it had worked out?
How different would I have been?

Saving myself

I slid down the edge
Of your darkened reality
Hoping to find your spark
Lost in your soul's city
The further I searched
I came to realise too late
I became consumed
Tangled up in your fate
Now I'm fighting two destinies
Still trying to save your soul's health
Whilst battling and losing
To save myself...

After getting the first line as a prompt from an amazing poet friend of mine, this seemed to spawn out of me.
I was transported back to times where I tried my hardest to save people from depressions grip only to get pulled into theirs and mine further.
This is part of the reason I write as well, so people can read and hopefully relate to my ongoing battle.

Choice

Deep into the broken midnight memory
He made a choice
He would no longer be a victim
And silence his voice
Anger is a powerful motivation
But regret is worse
The regret of always being broken
Lying in his hearse
As he ascended to the rainbow bridge
He seized one last look
Then unfurled his wings
And into the sky he took...

I wrote this as a nod to a past abusive relationship and the moment of realisation of when I decided enough was enough, I may put some more poems in here about that relationship so you can see it happens to men as well.

Praying

I'm praying to a god
That won't talk back
My faith is dwindling
I'm stumbling off track
Please hear my prayers
And send me a sign
Let me know you hear me
Or are my burdens only mine?
There used to be two sets of footprints
Walking through the sand
Now there's only one set
And on my own I stand...

Growing up catholic was hard for me as I got older.
Religion was pushed upon me and as I got older I started to question certain things.
One of my favourite poems is footprints in the sand and whilst I grew up believing it, I came to think that I was standing alone.

Another way

There is another way
So please put down the blade
You can fight against
Any choices you've made

There is another way
Please put down the knife
Turn the light on
And choose life

There is another way
Don't let the demons win
Please talk about this
And not keep it within

There is another way
A light at the end of the tunnel
Even if it seems all of the bad
Has made it down your funnel

There is another way
So put down the alcohol
Sobriety brings clarity
Without leaving you against the wall

There is another way
Let's step out of stealth
And create a safe place
To talk about mental health...

Lighthouse

It's alive
I shout with glee
I did it
Finally
I created something
That isn't only mine
She is a thing of beauty
And will shine
She will be a force for good
A harbour for lost souls
A shining beacon
And create new shoals
She will open her arms to all
Who need refuge and protection
Oh she will be a safe haven for all
Who have ever faced rejection
Oh my greatest work of art
You may be a building by the sea
But my little lighthouse
You'll shine for all to see...

It has always been a dream of mine to open a place for creative people of all ages, races and genders to come and create.
A safe place without hate or prejudice and a place for all the lost souls just looking for their lighthouse to guide them back to shore.

How?

How do I silence
My demons' tonight?
I desperately crave quiet
I'm losing this fight
How do I quench
Their undying lusts?
For my tears
As my metallic defence rusts
How do I extinguish
The fires they lit long ago?
Setting my soul ablaze
Fanning flames to grow
How do I gratify
Their sadistic urges?
Or at least survive
Until a hero emerges
How do I cocoon my paper heart?
And allow it to dry
Please tell me softly
How do I?

If, somehow, you have an answer to this almost rhetorical question, please find me on social media and let me know.

Goodbye

Tired of life and all its fuss
This kid stepped out in front of a bus
Now looking down from up above
He sees in this world he had no love
No one came to his funeral or wake
He knows now suicide wasn't a mistake
Happy ever after was a lie
He left with no goodbye
Neither heaven or hell to call home
He's stuck in purgatory alone
Forever wondering what could've been
Alas, what ifs, are no longer to be seen...

A fair few times I have found myself sitting with my demons and thought of no way out except death itself. One day someone suggested the Samaritans and I thought I'd just be a burden to them but I will always remember the first time I turned to them, it felt like a huge boulder had been lifted off my shoulders. Honestly, my friend, please find the courage to talk to someone, I say courage because it's definitely not a weakness to ask someone for help.

Infection

I cannot fake it
Not any more
Yes, I've cried in the shower
And laid prone upon the floor
Curled up hoping for peace
Drunk off another glass
My vision blurring
Will this pain pass?
My jester's face has slipped
It's long gone now
Forever lost
Can I survive somehow?
Or must I retire this smile?
And accept this dark rain cloud
As my only friend
Would that make you proud?
Is that what you want?
Submission to your taunts
Taking over my mind and body
As you infect my joints…

One of many conversations I have held with my demons, strangely enough I talk to them more than most people. I'm closer to beating them than I was but I still have a distance to go.

What the point?

What's the point if everything comes to an end?
Over time even ink runs dry from a pen
Memories eventually turn to dust
And the strongest metal rusts
Why can't certain things be immune to blisters
Like fathers, mothers, brothers and sisters
Why do we have to know pain or deaths?
Is this all part of God's test?
If it is then I give up and fail
Say whatever you want as you tell my tale
Say I was a quitter or a waste
But before you do, give my shoes a taste
Let's see if after a mile
You still walk with that smile…

I have sat in various places like coffee shops and park benches and wondered about this.
Do we know pain so we can know joy?
Do we know death so we know life?
It seems a little oxymoronic to me as the losses I've had over the years haven't made me feel alive, quite the opposite in fact.

Unkind mind

Nightmares again
Wake me from sleep
Inlay Wirth open eyes
Starting to weep
My skin is drenched
My mouths gone dry
I lay there wondering
Why oh why?
Another 2am shower
Doesn't clear my mind
Oh tortured brain
Why are you so unkind?

I have suffered from nightmares for as long as I can remember.
From watching exorcist as a child or when I lost my granddad, father and little boys (not at the same time).
I even had them when I spent a while in hospital and even as an adult standing on his own two feet, I still have them now.
I've written many poems about them but to this day I haven't ever seen anyone about them, maybe that's the next step?

Media

Trying to make it to heaven
By going through hell's streets
Currently playing the game of life
Full of only defeats
Everywhere we look there's war
Famine, Poverty and last breath
And yet you all wonder
Why some of us choose death?
Surely that's better than the eternal struggle
Of living day to day
Of living pay to pay
With nothing left to say
Except, Is there another way?

I regard myself as an empath so when the media only show me all the badness in the world I tend to feel the pain, sorrow and sadness of our world.

What happened to reporting good news?

Musical Influence

Boys don't cry
I guess you're The Cure
I love a waterloo sunset
You know my Kinks
I found somebody to love
She's my Queen
This is About a girl
She's my Nirvana
Hallowed be thy name
She's an Iron Maiden
She gave me a reason to fight
I guess I'm Disturbed
Before her I was a Wild Horse
I used to be a Rolling Stone
But with her it's a Beautiful Day
I really do love U2...

A different type of poem for you with a few of my musical influences.
Music truly has saved my life so many times, without music I wouldn't be here.

Tone

My head in my hand
A coffee in the other
Downing it quickly
Before ordering another
My notebook stares at me
The page left blank
My pen sees no action today
As there's nothing left in the tank
My mind has left me
Away it has flown
So please if you need me
Leave a message after the tone...

As someone who has grown up with ADHD (attention deficit hyperactive disorder), sometimes my mind completely deserts me.

Do you remember the old radios? When you tuned them and sometimes you'd hear static? That's how my mind leaves me at times.
In these moments my demons tend to win unless I drown them out with music and coffee but other times I'm too slow and they beat me.

Drowning

I was drowning
Slowly destroying myself
I was on a downward spiral
Due to my mental health
So out of the window
Went bad vibes
And in the front door
I built the best of tribes
Now I won't say every day is good
But I have umbrellas around me
I also have lighthouses
Guiding me from the sea
So to my tribe I say this
I see, hear and love you all
And I'll always return the favour
Should you ever fall...

Please, surround yourself in good people.
Negativity breeds negativity and positivist does exactly the same thing.
Build your own tribe full of people who only want good things for you.

Sometimes

Sometimes
The strong ones' break
Sometimes
They don't want to wake
Sometimes
The silent ones want to scream
Sometimes
They hope to wake from this dream
Sometimes
The angry ones want to cry
Sometimes
No tears come out when they try
Sometimes
They want it all to end
Sometimes
They just a friend
Sometimes
They want to quit for awhile
Sometimes
They actually smile…

What if mental illness was visible?

Would we treat it differently?

Have you?

Have you ever wanted to end it all in a day?
Wipe all the pain, tears and memories away
In an instant, thoughts of me will fade
When I reach for my razor blade
One swift cut and it all ends
With no goodbye to family or friends
I've never done anything bad
Yet I'm destined to be forever sad
I have no one to talk to or call
No one to pick me up after I fall
I'm getting tired of starting again
I just wish this pain would end...

I cannot stress this strongly enough, there is always someone to call and talk to.
In my darkest moments, when my poems (like this one) made me feel worse and not better, I turned to Samaritans.
They saved my life more times than I can count or recall.
Please reach out to them if you feel alone.

Stormy soul

There's this current
Flowing deep inside
Such a destructive force
From which I cannot hide
Sometimes I glide above
Windsurfing of sorts
But sometimes it drags me beneath
Knocking away my supports
Swept up in a maelstrom
A tsunami tide pinning
Each and every time
My defences are thinning
If you see me and I'm smiling
Know that isn't my norm
And just below my surface
A leviathan waits in his ravaging storm...

I have long believed my depression is just a mood I get in.
Now I know it's a deep rooted thing and part of me.
I'm still scared to get help though as I don't want to be ruled by drugs but I feel I may need to soon.

Place

Ever felt lost?
Ever felt alone?
Ever felt like a nomad
Without a home?
Not in the physical sense
But a place to feel secure
A place of warmth
A place that is pure
I'm hunting for this place
Searching far and wide
I need some where
Where I have no need to hide
A place to be at peace
A place to be free
A place for my soul
A place to just be me...

Sometimes a place isn't four walls, sometimes it's a heartbeat, a smile or even a cup of coffee.
I found my place in my notebook and a very big coffee cup.

Refund

To all the people
On whom I spent time
Helping you grow stronger
And become less of a mime
I need a refund please
Because I want my wasted time back
I need to use it on myself
And get back on track
So please return
My valuable hours
That I spent
Helping you recoup your powers
Just for you to fly off
And leave me stranded
And so I sit here contemplating
Completely empty handed
Hating myself for helping you
And being a friend
Just for you
To leave me in the end...

Don't ever be afraid or ashamed to put yourself first please.
Learn from my mistakes.

This is the last time

This is the last time
I message first
This is the last time
I wonder if I'm cursed
This is the last time
I cry in my pillow
This is the last time
I accept a no show
This is the last time
I'll be a doormat
This is the last time
I'll be treated like that
This is the last time
I swear it's true
This is the last time
Oh hey, how are you?

I always seem to give the wrong people too many chances, will this ever change?

Beast

On my soul
My demons feast
Today's question
For who could love a beast?
I mean
Is this my curse?
Destined to be alone
Even in verse
Have fairy-tales
Passed me by?
An unlovable man
In solitude I cry
Maybe one day
After the sands of time have shifted
I will finally have this curse
Lifted...

Are we ever as unlovable as we believe?
No one and I mean NO ONE is unlovable.

When

When a person
Loses their soul
No donor can be found
And slowly they lose control
When a person
Loses their mind
And takes their own life
Only then we start to be kind
When a person
Loses their heart
Imploding slowly
Could we have done our part?
When a person
Hurts them self
Isn't it time
We talk about mental health
Because when a person
Loses their fight
The world reacts
And shows them light
But can we be proactive
And invite free speech
Truly free without judgement
Maybe that will help us reach
Reach those needing it
Reach them before a blade
Reach them before the end
Before that final choice is made…

Let us talk

Let us talk about death
What comes after?
What happens next
Tears or laughter?
Should we mourn the passing?
Or celebrate life?
How can we be so progressive?
Yet not talk about strife?
Grief, mourning and depression
These subjects are taboo
Yet drink and drugs
These are okay to do?
What happened to the days?
Where it was good to talk?
Have we really progressed
When we only stand and gawk
Let us talk about the uncomfortable things
Challenge the status quo
And as a species
Let us continue to grow...

Someone once told me that only by talking about the uncomfortable things, can we become comfortable in them.
I didn't know how true this was until I knew what true loss was.

My Tale

Every day I cy
Every day I try
All that changes is the sun
Yet on the same course I run
In the light of day
I try, strive and pray
But in the darkness of night
My demons hold me tight
Unforgiving till sunrise
A quiet night is quite the prize
But my grafting shall never fail
And through my writing I'll tell my tale
And so I write
To bring to the light
My demons from the shadows
And allow this chapter to close…

I do hope I can always write, I urge you to find a passion and gift.

Peace

Laying my head on my pillows
Slowly my pain willows
I know tomorrow though it'll return
And on my heart it shall burn
Till one day I find peace
Or deaths sweet release
But will I be just as tormented as a ghost?
By the demons I fear most
Like the spectre of being alone
Or the phantom of sinking like a stone
Never reaching goals I've been set
Having the pain of expectations not met
These are my daily struggles, My trials
My endless journey, My 10,000 miles
I can no longer face this path of torment
Why can't my demons just lay dormant?
Against them I'm nothing and I fall
Until an angel answers my call...

I guess I'm just a broken man, looking for something to save me.

Soulless

Toxicity infects
Negativity brewing
Breeding inside
Slowly stewing
Infecting fully
Blackening soul
Poison destruction
Taking control
Contorting thoughts
Dreams decay
Destroying memories
Of yesterday
Happiness lost
Never found
Drowning alone
Without a sound...

Sometimes I think of the first line in a poem and something spews out.
Almost like something is guiding my hand.

Questions unanswered

My shadow of self-doubt
Blocks everything out
Except for the hate and disdain
Only adding to my soul's pain
Will there ever be a cure?
A way to become pure?
I'd do anything I could
To be seen ultimately as good
Will poetry be my tourniquet?
Or will I drown in this crimson decay?

I try to talk and words won't come out
I can only whisper when I want to shout
How do I vent without being called wild?
How do I cry without feeling like a child?
Instead whilst my lip is bitten
My words are left unwritten
Some poet I turned out to be
How can I save anyone if I cannot save me?

These questions are still being asked one poem at a time.

She's happy

A ripple in time
A memory long past
My melancholy heart remains
Fates hand rarely recast
Hugs long forgotten
A kiss still lingers
Oh heart why do you still ache?
Was she my one chance
Of an everlasting love
And whirlwind romance?
Then I wonder and hope
That she thinks of me
But then that passes
As I know she's happy...

Ah past love right?
I think that overthinking the what ifs in my life has contributed to my depression.
I'm learning to let these go, slowly.

Look at me

Look at my eyes
You'll see sorrow
Look at my smile
Dreaming of a better tomorrow
Look into my heart
You'll find it weak
Look at my mouth
You'll find it unable to speak
Look at my hands
You'll find them weathered
Look into my brain
You'll find it untethered
But look into my soul
You'll find a light
Burning luminously
Trying its hardest to fight
Take a step back
Now look at me
I wonder
What do you see?

Look in the mirror, what do you see?

I hope you see the fighter that you are.

Legacy

Plastic confidence
Ink filled veins
Stone hearted
Self-inflicted pains
Iron fisted
Barrel chested
Steel bones
Fully tested
Both natural
And man made
Ensure in time
I'll never fade
Wrapped in paper skin
With pens for fingers
Means long after I'm gone
My legacy lingers...

I want this book to be something good I have brought into this world.
If it becomes my legacy, then at least I have done something good.

Stars

We live under a sky of stars
Under a canvas of celestial lights
In a galaxy deep, dark and vast
Bringing us wondrous sights
We live in a system
Made up of wonder and grandeur
I stare up in wonderment
Hoping for a saviour
How? I muse to myself
In the vast vacuum of space
How miniscule my efforts
To put a smile upon my face
Does the universe care?
About someone so inconsequential
When even my own people exclude
And leave me rendered in a state of confidential
I also question if my salvation
Is tied to the cosmos or my own kin
Or do we just have to save ourselves
By looking within?

There are people to help but I do believe we have to begin with helping ourselves.
I could be wrong with the latter but there truly are people to help you.

Be kind

A person doesn't need water
To drown
A person doesn't need wings
To soar high
A person doesn't need to smile
To be happy
A person doesn't need to frown
To be sad
A person doesn't have to be scarred
To self-harm
A person doesn't need to cry
To ask for help
A person doesn't need to die
To gain love
A person doesn't have to suffer
To gain support
Everyone is fighting a war
That we know nothing about
So let us try being humans
And not dicks...

Do I need to say anything?

Church

My church is a bar
The waitress brings peace
She could easily be my vicar
Her drinks carry a release
The bartender offers confession
As I sit upon a barstool
He pours another vodka
The burn now feels cool
In this church
Demons go unchecked
Praying upon tortured souls
As another glass gets necked
The nearest to absolution
Is my vodka being absolute
I'm drinking to forget
But my memory is resolute
The jukebox kicks out hallelujah
The patrons sing and a few even cry
Yet this is a choir for the damned
And this our final goodbye
As closing time is called
Some of us won't see tomorrow
We all slink off alone
To drown in our sorrow...

I no longer attend this church or any other, my demons played too well with my drinks.

The choice: part one.

Picking this scab
The instant sting
It seems that pain
Makes my soul sing.

Now as this blade
Slices a fresh wound
The symphony in my soul
Has been tuned.

The claret river
Flows down my arm
My soul is dancing
To the devil's charm.

It seems this time
He has finally won
After this fatal slice
My after life has begun.

My world goes dark
I begin to cower
Standing before me
Three figures of incredible power.

One dressed in devilish red
One dressed in silky white
Ones dressed in pure black
Each makes an invite.

The choice: part two.

God's pitch is divine and pure
He speaks of salvation
An afterlife of service and atonement
For a reincarnation.

The devil makes a pitch
Telling me my soul is tainted
I've been tormented for so long
And on my soul his name is painted.

Death makes the final plea
He offers training
He'll mould me into death himself
A successor is who I'm destined to be.

I take a moment to decide
Churning over the bargains
I open my mouth to speak
"My answer is..." I begin...

The choice was written after I woke up in a sweaty mess and is based on a recurring nightmare I've had for over a year now.

I don't know why but I keep waking up before I make my choice.

Purely based on this poem, what would you choose?

Error 404

There's this flaw
Inside my code
Something has piggy backed
On my soul it rode
Infecting my motherboard
Rewiring my mainframe
Screwing my interface
Making me play its game
Error 404
Corrupted file
Forgive me
I only tried to smile
It seems happiness
Isn't in my programming
Am I obsolete?
Is my data jamming?
Do I need a reboot?
Or just a full clean?
I'm struggling to compute
I thought it was easier to be a machine?

Can I be a machine and feel for a while please?
Can I come with an off switch?

Unyielding

Lost at sea
No land in sight
Trapped below ground
Without any light
Surrounded by fog
Thicker than clouds
Isolated
Yet seen in crowds
Music playing
But only hearing white noise
Sleeping ruined
As negativity destroys
A beautiful sunrise
Peaking over the building
Another night survived
Against this battle unyielding...

Guess what? You survived again, please remind yourself of these little victories.

Did you know?

Did you know
It's okay to cry?
Did you know
It's okay to retry?
Did you know
It's okay to break?
Did you know
It's okay to not want to wake?
Did you know
It's okay to ask for a hand?
Did you know
A few of us understand?
Did you know
There are answers for questions you seek?
Did you know
It's okay to feel weak?
Did you know
It's okay to not be okay?
Did you know
It won't always be this way?
Did you know
I cry most nights?
Did you know
In my tunnel there's no lights?
Did you know
I've cut myself?
Did you know
I damage my mental health?
Did you know
Talking can help too?
Did you know
This was written for you?

For whom ever needs to hear this, It's okay to not be okay.
It's okay to start again.
It's just okay.

Insta-fame

Nobody wants to be nameless
Some people dream of being famous
How are you going to deal with the stress?
When all you can say is yes?
What's going to happen when you crack?
When life dumps you on your back?
Whilst your life starts crashing
Who's going to stop the cameras flashing?
Noting every move, you make
Picking up on every mistake
Yet you know you cannot moan
Wouldn't you rather stay unknown?

I used to always want to be famous on Instagram, I wanted my poems "liked" by thousands of people.
I still get caught up in the numbers game unfortunately but I do truly appreciate my few followers who take the time to read my stuff.
I've made them my poetic tribe and wouldn't trade them for fame any day.

Smiling on the outside

Oh lonely nights
I miss you so
Nowadays
My demons just won't go
They haunt me nightly
Leaving me crumpled on the floor
Curled up in a ball
At least I'm lonely no more
For they won't leave me be
Or let me dream of a happy place
Yet you'll never see this pain
As I have a smile upon my face
Outside it never slips
Faking it till it comes true
Whilst out in the public eye
What else am I meant to do?
And so I smile and may even whistle
Acting like everything is fine
Whilst upon my soul
My demons dine…

Does the phrase "fake it till you make it" apply to forcing yourself to look happy?
Or does it do more damage?
How long can we smile whilst our life crumbles?

Another nightmare

I stare death in the face
"Why can't I leave this place?"
I scream into its dark hood
"My boy, you're here for good"
Tears stream down my cheek
Damn when did I turn so weak?
Darkness envelops me whole
Consuming what was left of my soul
"How can I repent and be freed?"
I softly plead
Death places a hand upon my head
That's when I awoke drenched in my bed...

*I truly hate having a creative brain at times, it continues working even whilst I sleep and creates so many cruel nightmares.
Can we ever truly escape nightmares?*

Home

Home
Where I hear your laugh
Home
Where I run you a bath
Home
Cooking meals together
Home
Was meant to be forever
Home
Suddenly an empty space
Home
Where I no longer see your face
Home
With snuggles upon the floor
Home
A place that doesn't exist anymore...

Sometimes home isn't four walls and a front door.
Sometimes it is a heartbeat and pair of eyes.

Number one

I guess I'm not as strong as people think
I think of my life and my heart begins to sink
I cannot find the right words to explain
How it'd be easier to run from this pain
Start a new life far away
And start living for today
Hop on a boat and sail
All on my own without a tail
Just my notepad, my pen and my self
And start to work on my mental health
Fuck my career, off I run
It's time to look after number one...

So, I've tried this and failed.
Something keeps dragging me back to London.
Although I am planning another escape.
I hope by getting to know myself first will stand me in good stead.

Option

You treated me like an option
A plaything to fuck with
You made me believe in fairy tales
But they were just a myth
I was your clown to make you smile
Your knight at weak times
Your teddy bear to hold
And now judge of your crimes
You told me you liked me
Loved me you said
So how comes I'm alone
And you're with him instead?
You share laughter
And kisses galore
But who do you turn to
To pick you up off the floor?
Who do you run to in the dark?
Who do you stay with in the light?
So why do you turn to me
When you found Mr. Right?

I remember being this plaything for a "friend" and when I asked her these questions, I was painted as the bad guy. So I went and made myself a villain and now we don't talk anymore.
Not everyone we lose is a loss.

Void

I have this hole
I cannot fill
No matter how hard I try
With any amount of will
I've tried my hardest
But still it remains
As deep as a quarry
As vast as the savannah plains
It seems to be expanding
Will it consume me?
Or can I survive
And scramble to safety?
Is this how it ends?
Consumed by this void
Slowly imploding
Until I'm destroyed...

Does it, in reality, all end in a whimper and not an almighty big bang?

<u>Scars</u>

*You trace my skin
From scar to scar
Constellation making
From star to star
Quizzically musing
Which fantastic beast
I slay to gain them
Which one had its feast
My shoulders marked
By a giant minotaur
His claws running deep
Leaving me bloodied on the floor
My arms carry signs
Of a cosmic struggle
That time I flew too close to the sun
Just for a snuggle
Then you trace my heart
Tattered and shell hit
You make up another story
Without knowing it's because I'm a poet
Each time I pick up my pen
It adds more marks upon my soul
Spilling out onto my skin
As I wrestle for control
So you see, this is my battle
My eternal fight
My crusade against the darkness within
My quest for the light…*

My pen is my weapon but it hasn't always been this way I'm afraid.

Cleanse

I feel weak
Almost like quitting
I have this weight
On my soul sitting
I don't know to explain
This feeling inside
That when I'm around people
I just want to hide
I like people being happy
Making them feel at ease
But this takes its toll
It's hardly a breeze
But should I give up?
And not play the joker
Maybe I should don a straight face
Like I'm playing poker
Or do I carry on?
Despite the toll
Hoping one day
It'll cleanse my soul...

How do we cleanse? Prayer? Church? Drink? Drugs?
Writing? Making other people happy? Cutting ourselves?
Maybe it's a combination of these things?
Or maybe, just maybe, our souls aren't as dirty as we believe.

Mantra

Push boundaries
Break walls
Extend limits
Beat fools
Keep striving
Never slowing
Don't stop
Always flowing
Get bigger
Conquer doubt
Bring game
Let it out
Better yourself
Find a cause
Sing freely
Make applause
Inspire
Create
Stay true
You're great…

Repeat that last poem in the mirror.

Make it your mantra because you, my friend, are amazing!

I hope one day you will believe it and I truly hope it keeps you going even for one more day.

Stay strong my friend.

<u>Light</u>

There's this light
That I cling to
There's this light
Shining true
There's this light
Calling me
There's this light
Setting my heart free
There's this light
That bathes me whole
There's this light
That burns in my soul
There's this light
That keeps me going
There's this light
That keeps glowing
There's this light
It keeps me true
There's this light
My friend, it's you...

You, my friend, are the reason I have compiled this collection.
I truly hope and dream that you find your own light to shine your way through this horrendous battle.
Even though I may not personally know who you are, I understand this battle and recognise how strong you are.
Keep moving, even on the darkest of days, even if you stumble.
I won't give up on you.
I believe in you.

Printed in Poland
by Amazon Fulfillment
Poland Sp. z o.o., Wrocław